WAITING FOR THE NIGHTINGALE

Miles Burrows was born in Leicester in 1936 and educated at Wadham College Oxford, where he graduated in Classics, Philosophy and Medicine, having studied Russian in National Service. He did his internship at University College London and has practised as a doctor in the United Kingdom, New Guinea and in the Far East. He currently lives and works in Cambridge.

D0130093

Also by Miles Burrows

A Vulture's Egg: Poems

MILES BURROWS

WAITING FOR THE NIGHTINGALE

CARCANET

Some of these poems, often in rather different form, have appeared in the *Times Literary Supplement, Poetry Review, Poetry News, PN Review, London Magazine,* and *Ambit*. Special thanks are due to Alan Jenkins at the *Times Literary Supplement*, Maurice Riordan at *Poetry Review*, and to Martin Bax at *Ambit*.

First published in Great Britain in 2017 by
Carcanet Press Limited
Alliance House, 30 Cross Street,
Manchester, M2 7AQ
www.carcanet.co.uk

MIX
Paper from
responsible sources
FSC® C014540

Text copyright © Miles Burrows 2017

The right of Miles Burrows to be identified as the author of this work has been asserted by him in accordance with the Copyright, Designs and Patents Act of 1988; all rights reserved.

A CIP catalogue record for this book is
available from the British Library,
ISBN 978 1 784103 40 8

Typeset in Great Britain by XL Publishing, Exmouth, Devon
Printed in Great Britain by SRP Ltd., Exeter, Devon

The publisher acknowledges financial
assistance from Arts Council England.

Supported by
ARTS COUNCIL
ENGLAND

For Dr. Su-Fang Wu

'*Like certain animals under the influence of love, he felt the need of uttering a complaint.*'

Contents

In Dewar's *Himalayan and Kashmiri Birds*,
Songs of different species are set down clearly:
Soft, mellow *pee-ho* (Indian oriole)
A loud pleasant call of three notes: *Think of me* (Grey headed fly
　　catcher)
Loud, plaintive *pee-you pee-you* (Great Himalayan Barbet)
Melodious *Wherefore-wherefore* (Indian cuckoo)
Crescendo '*brain-fever* brain-fever, BRAIN-FEVER' (Large Hawk-
　　Cuckoo)
A loud, shrill '*Did he do it? Pity to do it!*' (Red wattled lapwing).

And we can imagine the wandering major in the foothills
Mapping out the shifting frontier posts
Disguised perhaps as a fakir with a goatherd's crook
Concealing measuring tape and a surveyor's protractor
And no doubt thinking, as brain fever descends on him,
About his own wife back in Hazelmere
With that awful car salesman type.

Meanwhile little is known about nightingales.
What do they do in daytime? Do they sleep?
Whatever we may think of John Keats,
He is little use to the birdwatcher in the field.

From melancholy I fled into the wood.
What plants could offer solace? Enchanter's nightshade
Was foisting withered berries like a stage apothecary.
What time was it? Midnight, and the anxious owl.

The *mise en scène* was almost reassuring
In its chill familiarity. Stepping back to avoid a shadow
I trod on a mandrake. And looking up at the full moon
Was rewarded by the sight of two marsh harriers

Flying high, playing and tumbling in courtship
Tossing a half dead mouse one to the other
High in the air. With a light heart
I looked round for my secretary:

'That is me, tossed between Love and Death, Harrington.'
I struggled back through a thicket, careful not to spoil my clothes.

PUSSYCATS

after Wyatt

They used to leave their stilettos by the door
As I recall, coming in barefoot to my study
In nothing but deerstalkers. Now they look away
Or even cross the street, as if *distrait*
Or they never knew me, or oblivious
Of the time when they opened their mouths recklessly
For my risky *canapés*, like tame pussycats.
Now, splitting up is cool. Mutability is the new black.
And Buddha said it's best to be detached.
Everyone has lost her memory, especially that one.
I'm let go with some vague understanding
Like an old retainer locked accidentally in a house up for sale
And treated with such *noblesse oblige*
That I'd give anything to see who she's ended up with.

1.

You will have time enough to sleep.
So get some practice now, you always need more.
Hold onto the penis tightly like
The stopper on a luke-warm hot-water bottle.
The other hand should be clenched like a fist over your mouth.
Relax and think of the happy times
You might have had.

2.

In Berlin for example. Somewhere you have never been.
You would surely have enjoyed it. In Berlin.
Eating German food. The hearty breakfasts.
You could have lived in Kantstrasse
And gone to work on a tram.
You could surprise people
By speaking words in German as you die.

3.

Or slip into Old Slavonic at the last.
Ask for *shchee.*
That'll give them a shock.
They'll come with banners and hampers,
Black headscarves, *pirozhki,*
Through the snow, out of the forest: sledges, horses' breath
steaming in the cold air.

4.

Afterwards, old men in felt-lined boots
Will walk back into the woods, taking snuff, talking about billiards.

My father would summon Doctor Wilkins
As he would summon my mother's dressmaker Picton Beyton
Directly to the house like tradesmen
Though in recognition of their being artists
They would come in at the front door
(At different times of course)
And have a glass of Bristol Cream in the lounge
Where the couch would be strewn with copies of *The Stage*,
Horse and Hound, and *Plays and Players*.
Doctor Wilkins, in that pre-Odorono period,
Would emanate a discreet suggestion of formalin
As if he had just returned from an autopsy.
Having viewed my toenail with unconcealed distaste
He suggested private referral to a specialist.
The strange thing was that Wilkins himself
(Known by his surname like the vet and the tailor
Though sometimes dignified with professional title
Depending on his performance) always wanted to be an actor.
For some reason I was once in his waiting room
And noticed in the glass fronted bookcase
A whole set of books on voice projection, posture, and gestures,
And facial expressions denoting different emotion:
How to dominate the stage but not too much,
Upstaging, and the different ways of leaving the stage while
sustaining a special effect
With what was called a 'slow curtain'.
Wilkins himself left no lasting mark on the theatrical world
Though with his moustache and small stature
He could have made a convincing stage detective.
Possibly my mother chose him as family doctor
Being herself a prominent amateur at the Little Theatre

Where she achieved good 'crits' in the Leicester Mercury
For her performance as a nun struck by hysterical blindness.
But she could never forgive him for taking a holiday in Madeira
In those days before air travel
As if he failed to appreciate
That the sacred bond between actress and devotee
Should never be broken by a moment's absence.

In a Sussex farmhouse before the war, simple ingredients in the
    rough
Were readily available (sunsets, owls, ferrets, wood smoke).
They required time and attention to process, yet were rewarding.
They are prized now by town dwellers who find them hard to obtain
And often only in processed or second hand form.
A lot of nonsense is written about *Form.*
Form is no more or less than shape.
The 1930s kitchen had its shapes cut out of tins
As moulds for trifles and junkets, themselves called moulds.
Have a few shapes and keep them clean and sharp.
Rhyme is no more needed than a two tone doorbell.
The reader is entitled to a *Theme:* e.g. loss, attraction,
Nausea, mystical union with nature. It is little use
Mixing themes (nausea with mystical union). Do not strive
For originality. Never lose contact with your reader.
Once lost it is hard, sometimes impossible, to regain.
Do not use the word 'gyre'. This can produce a severe reaction
In some readers. The same goes for 'desolate'. More importantly
Resist the temptation to introduce your poem
With a couple of lines from Dante. This will look
Like pampas grass in front of a 1950s terraced house.
Feeling: Standing in front of an old ruin (in Italy for example)
Can induce a poetic feeling in many English people.
Objective correlative: Having decided theme and shape,
Get hold of your objective correlative (see glossary page 47).
This could be a sunset, often a wild bird (e.g. a hawk, perhaps lame)
Or some obsolescent piece of country apparatus, such as a spade,
A dibber (perhaps belonging to your old father) preferably with
    some nostalgic flavour.
Old carpentry tools can often be found in car boot sales.
By contrast also try up to date materials like old betting tickets,

iPhones, tube tickets, deodorants, pizza packaging. With the right
  treatment
(prolonged whisking, montage) a 'sophisticated' dish can surprise.
But a reliable effect is produced more easily from ruined artefacts
And can rarely be beaten: an old Bakelite wireless or 'crystal' set,
A ruined Hoover (perhaps with torn bag or ill-fitting plug).
This is because many readers being themselves damaged
Or feeling damaged, or wishing to feel damaged,
Will identify more easily by means of the 'pathetic fallacy'
(See Chapter 10, footnote 37), though it is doubtful if this is really a
  fallacy,
Or they could be happy but still enjoy considering ruins in the same
  way
That we enjoy reading about murders or executions, floods,
  landslides,
Or people without enough to eat.

I dreamt that God was calling for me
By the wrong name. So I got into heaven
By using this wrong name. It was similar
To my name, but actually
Not mine, easily confused. Like the name
On my bus pass. As if
It was my name spelt backwards
Or jumbled up. As if perhaps
I had wanted to disguise my true name
And yet have it discoverable by anyone
Interested enough, at the same time
Difficult for the casual opportunist hacker.
Anyway I got in, met the old crowd.
– Howya doin'? Been a while.
– Doin' good. And Sheila?
And the people there smiled and looked
And continued talking in groups
Holding their glasses of ichor.
I wasn't convinced that they actually knew who I was.
I had hardly known them in college: they resembled
Memories of botany students, but not Daphne.
Was she there? Strange how love gets hold of you
By the nose and pulls you about
Like a provincial councillor in a Russian novel
Being pulled through a drawing room by a maniac.

THE SUMMERHOUSE

I've been reading a book about poetry.
It's complicated.
And mysterious designs on the cover.
You'd think she was writing about the origins of life
Looking down a spectroscope
To discover élan *vital*
In a summerhouse before term starts.
The poets appear like children
Dressed in enormous overcoats,
And they all belong to different schools
And are trying to tease each other. My school
Had a canary yellow blazer, and our crest
Was a summerhouse. (A Doric temple
The size of a phone booth). Other schools
Sported tigers, mailed fists, or griffons.
We brandished a summerhouse-
Symbol, Mr Rudge said, of effortless ease.
He was trying to produce a generation of small summerhouses
Some of which would revolve effortlessly,
Suggesting ill-defined juvenile longings.

Thick scales glisten below the Adam's apple.
And on the arms. I'm slowly changing
Into a crocodile. Like something out of Ovid.
I'm changing into Mum's crocodile skin handbag,
Expensive but completely out of fashion.
Always upstairs when it should be downstairs-
('It must be downstairs darling, could you look?') –
Impossible to find at the last moment – ('Maddening.
I must have left it upstairs. It's too hectic.')
I longed to be that handbag,
Centre of perpetual attention,
So elusive and effortlessly maddening,
Able to be upstairs and downstairs at once
And suddenly to manifest on Mum's lap all the time.
In old age, the crocodile skin handbag
Waits hiding on her lap beneath the table
And at supper, with an actor's smile,
She slips fresh scampi into its open mouth
To give later to the cat.

I live in a street of divorcees.
Mostly we're left to our own devices
Though one can be heard making love to Debussy.

The girl across the road's called Imogen.
Or so at least I should imagine.
She's become my oxygen, my Sanatogen.

The French would call it sexual anaemia
And others existential anomie
But she reminds me of a sea anemone

Or some marine anomaly
Flaunting her *vagula animula*
As casually as fine enamelling

And sets a problem that I'm slow to solve:
A solipsist unready to unselve.

The Mysterious Affair at Styles.
But this would be on a different shelf.
You could feel already the fine rain on the face,
Or worse, the sunlight dazzling you across the lake,
As you were *chargé d'affaires* at the F.O.
At the *Quai d'Orsay* or *d'Orphée*, or *Des Orphées* (or *Des Orphismes?*)
I determined to have an affair so I could end it.
But first I would have to become Roman Catholic.
I would need a suitcase for my underclothes, pyjamas and
    toothpaste
Or a valise, a thin novel for the train. A gold cigarette case. Discreet
    after shave?
I would meet her at Mass. At Brompton Oratory. Her hair covered in
    black lace.
Her family had been persecuted for ages and she'd been shut in a
    cupboard.
I practised genuflecting briskly to the left
While continuing to march forward without losing speed
(Remembering what I had learnt at ski-school)
And rapid Latin responses with a slight Polish accent.
And you'd defy the sinister Monseigneur
And the kindly old tipsy parish priest
And feel deeply anguished but have to go on with it
Like putting down your golden retriever.
You'd have to go on with it to the end
Though it would not be the end, more like
Never ending because the beginning had hardly been come to.
Everything finely balanced, it could go either way
Like soap in an eddy going out of the bath
Motionless at the edge of a maelstrom. The Foreign Legion
Would have to accept O level French. I practised
J'ai fait Le tour de LA tour Eiffel

She would be wearing a trace of elusive perfume
Like Mum's *Nuit de Noel*, or *Je Reviens*.
But shouldn't that be *reviendrai?*
Or is it I am in the process of coming back (making the journey
    back)?
Or *reviendrasse* (would that I had been about to come back?),
Or no perfume at all, though girls did sweat
Quite differently from boys. She would be a ballet dancer
Or a *cocotte* or a *grisette* or *demi mondaine*
Or even a courtesan, though that was mainly in Ancient Greece.
I smoked *gitanes* in the woods by Frensham Ponds
With Ladbroke-Coutts. If only our family
Lived in Chester Square or Tite Street, not in Leicester.
Or could have a signet ring with a crest on it.
Dad could go hunting as much as he liked
But we remained hopelessly provincial. I blamed my father for this.

At this age it would surely be better
(Rather than waking at 2 A.M. holding the penis)
To be writing a Chinese poem
Of the T'ang period
About being a civil servant
Banished to some tedious monosyllabic province
And watching the leaves rustling
On the neglected threshold
Of a summerhouse, the paintwork peeling,
A pair of thin cranes breasting the featureless sky,
Trying to remember the days when Rachel would come round in the
    afternoons
On her bike
While I was trying to get on with my novel
And the poem itself could be a T'ang horse
Done in the 'drunken flight' style of calligraphy
Using a dry brush.

Even the Ming period would do.
As if the poem was an unwieldy blue vase
Of uncertain provenance in the auction rooms
Of a country house, the kind of vase a child might have been sick
    into
After a wedding. Or you could even translate it
From Chinese into Russian, seizing the opportunity
To introduce the delightful word *shelyest*
For the rustle of dry leaves.

So he had to take a run
Like a fast bowler.
I could have been Sir Walter Raleigh
Kneeling on the chair like a scaffold
And crossing my legs piteously.
I had been beaten more times than Dr Johnson.
If I was beaten any more I might know enough
To write a dictionary. Dictionaries were what set us apart from
    animals,
Though our Labrador could carry the Telegraph.
I felt punishment must be improving me
And asked if I could be beaten again to save time
Instead of gardening.
Mr Penge (despite his love of *Kindertotenlieder*)
Was incensed at this suggestion.
But I needed to improve to get to Oxford for the accent.
We had to memorise the colours of house ties.
Hollinger's were forget-me-not blue on indigo, while Punter's
(Where Parkin minor lived) were gold and Vallombrosa stripes on
    sepia.
(You had to know the exact shades.)
There were seventeen houses and each had two ties
So it followed there were 357 combinations
Because each house had two housemasters. For example:
If Mr Utteridge wore a gamboge stripe on violet
What would he be disguised as, on a Thursday?
A mushroom tie with maroon and ochre stripes
Was Benker's and not generally respected as they played tennis
And Mr Pickering had married his housekeeper.
Mauve on Venetian pink meant you were Scrode's
And could put at least one hand in your pocket.

I dreamt the bus was going to Arcadia
And I was Death and I had missed the bus.

Uncle was to be cremated
At Gretna Green. It was to be
An elopement in flames with the Italian widow
He used to have lunch with in the Italian restaurant
Opposite the Army and Navy Stores
Where they put too much water in the Campari
And he greeted the waiters in Italian
But they did not recognise him.
Finally among three synagogues
A cloister appeared looking out on a golf course
And carved with the names of famous chefs.
Uncle as an old India hand
Would surely have been pleased
To share an incinerator with the Maharajah of Cooch Bihar.
Later, we walk to Novellino's down a side road,
Lamenting the loss of the King James version.
They never use it these days, it's hopeless.
Bert's looking after someone's yacht in Greece. Aubrey
Is in pirate insurance so has had to dash.
Outside the restaurant on the pavement
Grappa out of polystyrene mugs
Avoids corkage. It's mushroom *bruschetta*.
Lucinda orders a *macchiato*. We copy her
As she seems to know what she's doing.

No amorous descant this morning?
The birds silently open a dream through a gate of rain.
I bury my face in a pile of child's clothes.
Your letter is short and to the point.
I don't think you should go into a convent.
But anyway that's really your own decision.
I don't think I should try to influence you.
Today I am going to read all the books in the library.
It's going to be a big job as it's on six floors.
I will start in the alcove of Polish music.
The sky is blue now. They are opening the library,
The birds still quiet, having missed the half-light.

I have got as far as Transcendentalism
And it's still not coffee time.
I don't understand the Dewey system
But make a tiny mark on books I've read so I don't read them twice.
Reading a book no one's read before! Footsteps in snow!
Scott in the Antarctic, wondering if you'll ever get back
Or will people come and find only a half eaten dog,
A half empty jar of Cooper's marmalade. Some of these alcoves
You could be in a tributary of the Amazon in your pirogue
And wondering if you'll ever disembogue.
In Rare Books a man comes out with a monocle
Which allows him to read tiny handwriting and makes him lurch
    unsteadily
Looking astounded as Patrick Moore discovering a new planet.

I lost my small poetic craft.
It foundered in the water
With Nero's collapsing wedding boat
And the sea king's daughter.

I did not know my fore from aft
But tried to strike a cheerful note
By reading *Kulturwissenschaft*.
Now seaweed is my overcoat.

My wedding bed is understaffed.
I lost my religion at the Tote
And couldn't get an overdraft.
Now I'm a cub reporter.

My head's in the water, my head's in the air
And yet I'm not Apollinaire:
Ah non mon petit frère
Au mien crepusculaire
Cracquelant de savoir faire.

The single bar electric stove
Will teach us all we need of love
And how the constellations move.

A woman is doing her embroidery in the converted chapel.
And there is Priam in his seven-walled city, look,
That tumbles over the Umbrian hill like golden syrup.
And who is that stumpy figure
Hopping on one leg? Rumpelstiltskin?
Crows punctuate the sky. And as she dozes
The figure opens its mouth as if to cry
Or drink. In his lapel two poppies,
Remembrance and Oblivion. In her mind
He is saying this, though not in speech.
– Think Dunkirk in reverse
With half the boats and twice the angels
Not all of them guardian. Our mission was
To rescue that young woman for Burne-Jones
And bring with us the first slave owning democracy
In the Western world. At the time, Empires were collapsing
With the demise of domestic service. When 48%
Of butlers had the equivalent of an MSc in sociology
It was time to take the gilt frames off *The Voyage to Cythera*.
We went out there with attitude. We knew
Helen was being patronised by old men twittering like bats.
There could be a run on the drachma. Where was Onassis?
Everyone needs his Dardanelles.
I had a photo of Penny back in Suffolk
And missed the teenage years of my son
But looking back with hindsight
I'd say we had the balance right, because
The future's in the past and this was now.
We were fighting for Byron, Stowe, the Elgin Marbles,
The survival of the Classics Department
For Regent's Park Crescent, Euston Arch. Sooner or later
We were all going to be dug up by Schliemann.

His wife would try on our funeral masks.
We were very chilled, very focussed, looking forward to it.
When we got back, people couldn't understand
How we could pre-date Hotel California.
Déjà vu was a coffee bar. Everyone was dancing *Ceroc*.
Steeped in antiquity like old tea bags, we were used by art students
To smear on cartridge paper for a distressed finish.
They needed us for that.

I LONG TO TALK WITH SOME
OLD LOVER'S GHOST

I would not like to talk with some old lover's ghost
At all. Imagine: there he is, the old lover
Sharply dressed in tweeds, shooting his cuffs,
A lady's man, twinkle in his eye,
G & T at hand, tapping his cigarette against the case
Before inserting it into the amber holder, eyes aglow.
It could be your wife he is thinking of,
This smooth ticket burnt by a shooting star.
Seagulls crying over Brighton
Can be heard from the lounge bar of the Old Ship Hotel.
Old lovers are too much with us already.
Some are in prison, others on the stage.
You'll hardly get a word in edgeways
As he drops the names of people you never heard of
In a little restaurant where you can't see what you're eating
Till you spit out part of a hen's pelvis.
Lovers imagine Metaphysics
To be some kind of baroque fire escape
That lets them change the subject
While continuing to talk about themselves.

Henry and Margaret were buying an old church.
Henry said it had a Wow factor.
He liked it more than he could say.
He could put his computer in the old – chancel, was it?
The staircases were top spec. Fantastic floors.
Margaret was not put off by the graveyard at all
And felt she could certainly do something with it
To make it match up to their requirements.
She could just see her guests gazing up to where
The architect had put the granny-flat
While preserving the pulpit as conversation piece.
The font was wittily converted to a shower
And in the mezzanine stained glass at knee level was a definite plus.
The leper hole made a convenient serving hatch.
The only problem was: it was a semi.
You could either own the graveyard or the tower.
Tough choice: or could they stretch to both?

I originally wanted to be a witch
Sitting inside a Leiden jar
In the pathology museum
Or manifesting suddenly in a tallboy
Or a trick of light in a motorway café.
My fall back application
Was to be one of those nuns in *La Dolce Vita*
In an enormous starched wimple
Like the collar of Philip II
As if my head was something that had fallen into a serviette.
I wanted to be Dr. Zhivago
And pull a Russian mistress on a sledge.
There are no crosswords in heaven
Because there is no tomorrow for the answer.
Later, psychiatry took my fancy.
I wanted to rescue an enchanted mad princess
From a tower in a wood
Where the Senior Registrar was making curry.
I hoped to meet some brilliant eccentric
Cataloguing shadows or decanting clouds like Harpic
Into old sherry bottles.
The works of Freud were like a very long
Businessman's lunch in a German restaurant in Charlotte Street
Where the waiters have aprons going down to their ankles
And there is only one course on the menu but it is very good.
I was looking for an Irish country house, Grade II listed
Set in parkland, where the Medical Director
Organised an annual rough shooting party
For the staff to take potshots at each other
From behind haystacks
While inside the building huge women sat in stone circles
And we taunted them like boys taunting a dolmen

Or the Persian king whipping the sea.
Sitting in the water-tower on night duty
Waiting for the arrival of the princess
I found further philosophers plied their antique charms.
Binswanger, Glogg, Jaspers, Heidegger, Snoek
Opened their swing doors to me
Like bistros in Charlotte Street with irresistible names
And I would conjure with their smoky names
Savouring their names like Italian ice creams
Or like a harpsichordist
Who slowly releases his fingers from the keys
And looks up at the candlelit ceiling
As if the music were someone he had left behind.

I trained for a psychiatrist at one time.
It wasn't bad as a job but the food was terrible.
They brought it round in a thing like a Bessemer converter
On wheels, a galvanised iron vault like something
Edgar Allen Poe was frightened of being buried alive in
By accident. It had a thick wire coming out of it
And was connected to the mains. Sometimes one of the research psychs
Would say: The soup – is really not too bad today, David.
(David was the name of the hospital director:
He was the paratroop style of psychiatrist
And would sit on his chair like an ejection seat on a Tornado and he'd say
– It is, as you say EXCELLENT soup! At which the research psych,
Always a stickler for accuracy, would say
– I didn't actually say it was excellent soup.
Which sounds fatuous but was brave in the circumstances.) We ate
In a room with no windows at all, like a diagram
Of part of the cerebellum in a child's encyclopaedia
Where little people sit inside the intestines
Pouring acids and alkalis and operating telephone switchboards.
There was a white tablecloth and glasses, like the setting
For a play by Strindberg. The telephone was half broken
From its wall bracket, as if we'd wanted to vandalise it,
To cut off, here at any rate, all communication
Between ourselves and the patients. We'd had enough
All morning of dressing up, pretending to be indistinguishable
Because here it was lunch time and lunch was sacred.
A little old lady pops her head in again at the door.
Bradshaw is the only man to voice the general feeling.
– GET OUT! OUT! OUT! He roars. They liked him best.

Better to be writing your will again,
To be feasting in the great hall by firelight
Playing the harp to your grandchildren.
What is that terrible cry at the end of the garden?
It has gone now.
Could have been birds. Wild geese perhaps.
Let your trembling hand draw an expressive line.
Consider the scuffs on the risers to the stairs,
The dent of the doorknob hitting the wall
Always at the same place. Unpurse your lips:
You are not writing prescriptions.
Nor falling downstairs in a foreign language.
Practise the smile of the Indian swami.
Relax, your rivals are dead.
At least you're not in a Mexican motel.
Hang up the picture of a Chinese sage
Sweeping things under an enormous rock.

How many beads are left the nuns won't tell
(No no, my honey pie my honey ange!)
The hounds on Faustus' tail no longer bell:
Ranter's at breakdown point, Ringwood has mange.

Inflated *aves* tinkle smaller change
And cook is angry that the shapes won't jell:
If Sister Sycorax is acting strange
Joss-sticks may hide what candles cannot quell.

Mother Superior has plans to sell
Mount Carmel and prospect a different range.
Linda will take us on her Caravel
But who will babysit the stock exchange?

God's camera's zooming in on Brimstone Grange:
In the producer's eye – not you as well?
How many beads are left the nuns won't tell:
Their *aves* never tinkled smaller change.

You've never visited the city?
But you must have seen pictures. You must go there.
People go in buses, even nuns.
It affects the way you cook.
You've been to lectures by Freischutz
About the trapdoors for releasing panthers?
A city with brochures and folding maps
Mostly mythical, with an underlying fascist element
Disguised by warm expressive mannerisms,
Illegible graffiti and defaced politicians
Where two bearded youths in Hombergs sit facing each other
astride railings
Deeply French kissing at noonday forever without taking their hats
     off.
Its underground system and terrible fountains,
Its petrol stations controlled by six-legged dogs.

'You're not in love with me,' said Melanie Buckmaster, readjusting
    her things.
'You're just in love with something in your own mind.'
People always said that. (Moira Hardcastle had said the same
In the zoological museum, standing beneath the skeleton of a giant
    whale).
How could they know what was in my mind or what it corresponded
    to?
Had I called out some different name in my sleep?
If I had asked her for supper and we had arrived all dressed up
And climbed carpetless stairs to an empty room
With no orchestra, not even a guitar or a sound system,
No candlelight, no discreet clattering from the distant kitchen,
No fragrance of pesto or that other stuff
They put on Italian food, no crisp white tablecloth, no table,
No waiters in long white aprons down to their ankles,
Not a chair or even a stool to sit on, no curtains on the window, a
shadeless bulb,
And then said, 'How would you like to start with a drop of Frascati
While we choose? They say the Hungarian duck is very good,'
Then she'd have cause to look at me like that.

Another method is called the theatre of memory.
If you want to remember the name of your first girlfriend
(And not everyone wants to do this)
You construct in your mind's eye a house
In the Millington Road area as you're not paying for it
And then wander through this house and all its rooms.

You can even get some construction work done while you are
wandering
Calling her by name or by other names if you're not sure.
You can also look in the cupboard under the stairs
As they are often hiding there, and may even leave the light on
Shining through holes in the door into the dark corridor even in
    midsummer
Which is the time of year you are likely to be doing this.
You go in, and – Beryl?
Is not actually there but it feels as if she has just left.
The nudes painted inside the cupboard door by Francine
Have long since been painted over in furious white gesso by Romola?
And the books on – ('what's this? Tantrism?
We'll see about that. I'll need this cupboard for tools') –
That were there are now
Screwdrivers, hammers, tins of nails
Ranging from 3-inch plaster nails to 1/8-inch gimping pins
Inside Swiss herbal cough lozenge tins which are themselves
Inside old bags of Thai rice in woven plastic.
A Russian poetess could have lived in here with a partner
If they were on shift work
And they could discuss the use of broken
lines
to suggest nerv-
ous-

breathlessness
Or like
people
on TV panting dram-
atically as they clamber
up cast-
les on seacoasts.
Corfe Castle!
Maureen!
In the sheepskin coat with the collar up.

Thank you for your question, Gavin.
The problem was, then, that the house was infested
By people who had never been your girlfriends
And never would be.
Like Alessandra's elder sister Consuela
A tall doe eyed girl from Italy
Who said Open the Waters
As if she was a Handel oratorio
When she meant turn on the tap.
They are all there, living their own lives,
Not recognising you as landlord,
Disdaining to pay any rent and scorning housework,
Just standing around in the Millington Road area
Decoratively
Draping themselves against brooms in doorways like models.
Well thank you for that Gareth
But we're running out of time.

I was reading *Poetry of the Committed Individual*.
The girl at the bar was reading *Structural Anthropology* upside down.
The man at the table was reading *Confident Salesmanship*.
I was dreaming I was A.E. Hemingway.
But who was A.E. Hemingway?
That can't be right, even in a dream.
Above the Buddha, a garland of browning jasmine.
You are my horse, my Tang horse.
She leads you by the nose.
Et branle, branle, branle charlotte.
Don't give me flowers. I thought it was sad, those young girls.
You can tell he's going to kill himself.
You can feel it in the first paragraph. As if he's talking in his sleep.
The rhythm, the repetitions, the dust on the roads.

Timing in love: what a theme for the novelist!
The wasp-orchid looks pretty nondescript
But smells like a virgin wasp just out of the bath
(And, this is the point, is always on time).

Now the actual teenage virgin wasp is in no hurry to get out of the
    bath.
ENTER the Young Male Wasp. Beside himself with desire,
He plunges blindly into the aroma of the orchid
(Which happens to be standing close by in a state of readiness).
He emerges covered in pollen and the indelible illusions of
    romance.

Three weeks later, the real virgin, having overslept,
Finds her body-odour all over the bathroom
And the young male turns stupefied eyes towards her
Like a novel-reader at the tennis club
Who hardly sees the girls on court, being still half stunned
By his life-changing brush with Mme Chauchat.

Buy me some duck.
Going for a shower in her wraparound.
It's finished. I'm not going. I'm through.

No, no. If you get a letter you must go.
Going for a shower in her wraparound.
And Dick? What will happen to him?

You don't need a visa to commit suicide.
He could become a bonze.
Western Civilisation is finished. Finished.

If all the *farangs* could go home. Give them a little land, like Nam
    Zhou –
They could farm, breed horses. French Guiana?
What do you think then? A little risqué?

O hoho wowo yeyeh yeyeh
The sun peeps over the ridge. On the skyline three stricken trees.
The generator starts like an outboard engine.

A rifle fires twice. Single unsilenced shots.
A shot replies from a different weapon
Better silenced, high pitched, faster.

The generator stops, unveiling the cockcrow.
Children crying, and the sound of a lorry
Moving fast up the hill to Laxmai.

THE BATHERS

After Seurat

You have to believe other people exist.
Like the Holy Ghost,
It would become clear later.
A book about the carpentry of crucifixion specified mortice joints,
Chamfering, balance points, guide ropes.
You would most likely die of not being able to breathe properly.
That three headed dog on your way to the lavatory
After lights out, you knew its name,
And people each twisting inside his special torture like gym
    apparatus.
Truscott alone in the empty bathroom,
His raven hair and ivory skin naked in the moonlight
As he balanced himself on the edge of the empty bath,
Arms outstretched, dreaming of crucifixion.

I walked on past, tooth-mug in hand
To the mahogany lavatory. People exist because they get in your way
Ahead of you in the queue in the break
To see Doreen undressing in the wendy house.
I thought it was a queue for milk.
People in slums had to be helped.
Theoretically. Or if you became a missionary bishop
In Fiji where they played cricket.
A long way to go to find yourself in a cricket team
Unable to hide in the long grass.
To be conscripted as umpire,
Wearing sweaters tied round your waist.
Mum was always going out to the theatre
Flashing Stream (Highbrow). Don't kiss me darling I've got a cold.
And pretend to forget our names. Mrs Trench
Ate through a whole box of Cadbury's milk tray

With a glass of water. Including the bottom row.
People came up all the time in history, on French banknotes
Running after a woman with more than half a breast coming out,
Like Nurse Pinkney in her borrowed bathing costume
When the big wave came up at Trearddur Bay. We didn't look.
And people who hadn't been to our school (even one of our masters
    hadn't actually)
I wouldn't mind being married to a Javanese woman in the
    encyclopaedia
Or the girl in the brassiere advertisement that I traced out
And keep on my bedside table with Dennis Wheatley.
Or Caroline in the Sunday Dispatch in the wood with that French
    officer
Half fainting on the moss while people scrummed round the table
And Rossiter in his special polio boot skidded backwards into you
    from the pingpong table
at high speed
Successfully retrieving a deep smash.

K.J. Elderman, FAMILY BUTCHER,
Had an establishment at the corner of Holbrook Road
That gave this part of Romsey the look of a *quartier*
With its awning, its blackboards of chalked offers
And the blue striped aprons, white pork pit hats.
There was an atmosphere of joviality
Among gossiping housewives, excited
By so much raw meat cut from different angles.
Bethany and I were 'seeing' each other
Or at least I was looking at her a lot
Through a haze of cigarette smoke and Tibetan Buddhism
And I popped in here for a pound of ham for lunch
While Bethany hovered in the doorway in her jeans.
Elderman sliced the ham, nibbling small bits
In his usual way, and handed it to me, wrapped
In greaseproof, with a twinkle and a wink.
As if he saw this episode in my life
Sketched not by Graham Greene as I'd supposed
But Alan Ayckbourn. Who knows what a butcher sees
From his window? I never went back.
Till decades later I wander in here again
And he slices the ham, nibbling a few offcuts,
And hands it to me
As if shy of putting the question into words.

Mr Pin the tailor,
Known to my father as Pin or Pinny or even Pinniboy,
Owned an establishment on the London Road
Near the L.M.S. station, between an auctioneer and an estate agent.
Why don't you let me get you a suit at Pin's?
Dad would say towards Christmas.
I would remember the little hallway, very dark
Darker than any consulting room, and the door off to the right
Into a little room like a studio
Where a torso wore a tweed jacket
And Pin's cutter would come out of a further room still
And you could browse through tweeds bound in leather quarto
Or if it was too hard to choose
You could take them away like thick library books.
Dad would often choose the largest checks
As these were hardest to copy ready made
Or off the peg,
Would toy with enormous squares half the size of a man's back.
Later, at Oxford, a socialist,
Yet not wanting to disappoint my father,
I'd ask Pin to try to make my suits look ready made.
Till then I'd chosen in innocence
Heather and Donegal
And worn them tight fitting under the armpits,
Snug fitting as Pin would call it,
Tight as a fingerprint,
Tight as a social half-nelson.
Pin specialised in hunting attire
And the shop was full of hacking jackets hanging up to be cleaned
With the names of hunting people with titles.
We called Dad the pantomime baron
When he came into the kitchen in his black boots

But he galloped away in them
Till he won his hunt buttons,
Something else for Pin to sew on.
And once he gave me an old suit of his
Made of a very rare obsolete material,
Ginger herringbone with a check in turquoise and emerald
Valuable as a lithograph when the stone is broken.
Yet somehow I imagined
That in this labyrinth there were further rooms still
With other possibilities,
Detectives' outfits hanging up to be cleaned
With the names of well-known sleuths,
Spies' astrakhan overcoats,
The huge leather aprons of Victorian surgeons
And somewhere even
The yellow oilskins and thigh boots of an arctic fisherman.

If you had something to say
You should say it concisely,
To the point, and so clearly
I would hardly know you were speaking.
A good poem is like a well-made English suit.
You hardly notice I'm wearing it till I've gone
And you have a faint feeling of having missed something

Chidswell is gone. Despite his powerful serve and knowledge of
    Swedish.
Culloty is gone. Despite his Life of Blok.
Skivington is no longer seen in the queue for fish.
And where is Furlough?
They keep you alive now. Uncle Ed was 90.
He thought the nurse was a cabin steward.
Madeline spoke a few words in schoolgirl French
Believing she was on a ferry to Dieppe.
Putting the phone down, I keep clearing my throat
As if to make a speech. And there's Dad coughing nervously
In *Halcyon*, checking centre-plate and stop watch
As we bear down to the starting line
Upwind of *Cormorant*, listening for the gun.

The next poem we can't actually see.
In fact it may not be there at all.
But if it was there it would solve several problems
In the poems that we can see. We infer its existence
From what we believe to be its effects.
It may be a completely new kind of poem
Or something similar, that has leverage
On existing poems, being itself unreadable
And extremely heavy and moving at a high speed.
Heavy invisible rapid poem-like entities
Which may never be seen or felt, almost certainly underlie
Existing poems, and may outweigh them
As the dead outnumber the living.
And they have an activity, as the dead
Can bend existing poems and hold them together.
But these are not dead poems
(We haven't got a name for them yet).
They may explain shivering, wrinkles, or otherwise unexplained
    anomalies
In poems we thought we understood. Lacunas,
Leanings, hesitations, small lapses in grammar, odd coinings,
Unexplained dashes or ashes where commas might be expected,
A wandering semicolon. Misspellings we pretended to ignore.
Two instances of *hapax legomena* in seventeenth century Siamese
    poems
Could be explained by a heavy unwritten poem-like entity (about
    the size of Denmark)
Passing rapidly very close to them or through them.
In fact the whole field of textual criticism
Has become much more exciting
As we study here underground in darkness and close to absolute
    silence
Poems we thought we remembered.

I could write a biography.
Of myself.
Or even of some different person.
But who else might be of interest?
Nelson has been done so many times.
They could make a pillar for me
And I would scorn the pillar
And be simply lying down on my back relaxing
At the base of the pillar
Eating some olives from a back-pack
And wondering what the time was.
And people would look and say
'Are you one of those people who dress up as a statue?
Is that grey paint sprayed on? Is it toxic?'
'Not at all. People think I'm Lord Byron
But actually it's Christina Rossetti;
I can do a good Charlotte Mew
But not today. I'm not up to it'.
'You're like the dead girl in the wrenched-open coffin
With her grey dead baby, when Julie Christie
Asks Terence Stamp "Do you love me?"
And he says "She is more to me
Than you are, or were, or ever could be."
How old are you? What's it like being a dead poet?'
'It's very like being a live one:
Trying to play the piano
With breakfast honey still stuck between your fingers.'

Everyone in our street is doing Feldenkreis.
In the evening we go to watch Cymbeline in Finnish,
Followed by a workshop for women on shamanic drums.
We queue for fish at the corner.
Then it's power-walking with the Irish wolfhound.
Old ladies dress like Latvian peasants.
My neighour's garden sports Mbrumgu prayer sticks.
The other side's just back from Ascension Island.
Virginia Woolf's aunt used to live across the road.
Everyone is playing an upright piano in the front room.
Some of the front gardens have olive trees.
(Where would the good life be without Italy?)
Small children in Peruvian hats
Hurry to school carrying miniature cellos.

In the days when girls' names
Were postage stamps to unlikely countries
Persephone Finch was my blue Guadeloupe.
Her face in the college photograph
A daisy in a graveyard.
The boater floated like an aureole.
I followed her *au pas de loup.*
She played real tennis
(Not recognised by our tennis club,
Being played by Henry VIII
With a triangular racquet).
Walking Deirdre round the meadows, I gathered flowers
But threw them away, thinking of real tennis.
The tennis I played began to seem unreal.
So I changed religion.
If I was from an old Catholic family, with a real tennis racquet,
Would I be up to scratch?
Later, at an Elizabethan restaurant above the Chaplaincy
We ate marchpane together by candlelight
(With stuffed sow's wombs, as they also did Roman cookery)
And discussed the Neoplatonism of Professor Zvov.
Her accent was irresistible
But then so was Professor Zvov's,
Especially when he said *Pico della Mirandola.*

EMPIRICAL SONNETS

The Road to Krakow

'Are you an academic?' She says,
'You dance like an academic.
I'm being hauled about like a sack of potatoes.'
She goes white and has to sit down in a different room.
'It's like riding a donkey on Brighton beach.'
So I say, 'Do you go to Brighton a lot?'
I've got so old my wife can only go out with me after dark.
Another cramped little poem in its little seat-belt.
So I go to this psychiatrist.
'I think things are funny which are not funny.'
'You're not mad,' she says. (I could tell she was hopeless.
I could see from the pictures she hung on her walls.
'I don't like walls hung with reproductions,' I say.)
'They're originals,' she says. (So it's worse).

So I organise a getaway minibreak to Krakow.
Jessica says: 'That's fine. I'll organise it.
Midweek senior citizen rail supersaver to Stettin
Via Lodz before 28th dep Luton 0330 in a group returning
In time for you to be back at work on Friday.
'But I wanted Krakow.'
'You don't want Krakow. When you get to these places
All you do is drink coffee. You don't need to go all that way
To drink a cup of coffee. I'll buy you some coffee
And we can make it and drink it here. Why Krakow?
'I want to hear Polish girls talking Polish.'
'Play Chopin. Shut your eyes and you're in Krakow.'
'Yes! It's better than Krakow! (But I'd still like to see Krakow.)'
'Why? No. I want to understand your mentality. Why?'

1.

In the gap between two chairs, there is no third chair.
If there was a third chair, there would be no gap.

2.

In the gap between meals, there is the snack.
Between the poem's words, we imagine the snack,
Unable to wait for the next word.

3.

Some animals graze all the time. (Plankton, Buffalo.)
They are grazers. There is no gap.
Does their life have no meaning?

4.

There are gaps in birdsong. Meaningful,
As we may say 'she closed the door pointedly.'
But the birds are still preening, gathering twigs.
They sleep with eyes open, imagining gaps in their dreams
So that gaps still occur, and the gaps in the song have character,
A relief after chiselling at the dawn.

5.

An artist fakes an antique fragment and buries it under a lawn.
This is called the cult of the fragment.

6.
Somepoetssavingpaperleavenogaps
Their creations are swipecard numbers
Making sense only to another secret poem
Known only to the poet and his friends.
The poem is the gap into which the key is inserted.

7.
People are always crying out for meaning
Like a piece of small change that is being withheld.

And when you finally get to the place
Hiring a local Zif, declining with some regret
The services of the blonde chauffeur
In her well cut handwoven tweeds,
And drive yourself over the humpy bridges
That link the different islands of the settlement,
Passing the terrible prophets, and the cave
Where they make crayons and nobody mentions
The name of the local artist (nor is he recalled
In any street name or piazza), you pay
To enter the Jewish cemetery and look in vain for his name
As you can't read Hebrew nor the local lettering
Unrelated to Cyrillic or Lithuanian, and was he a Jew?
You proceed on foot into the gated private road
(Sneaking through with the armoured water-trucks)
Past old men in vests and short trousers and sandals
Smoking as they sweep in front of their apartment blocks
While Irish wolfhounds hurl themselves against the reinforced glass
Of the French windows as you pass by, already tipsy
From the local blueberry liqueur.
You walk backwards and forwards over
The nine bridges connecting the eleven islands
In a way that is mathematically insoluble
And take instructions from a wounded ant, a struggling bumblebee
And a lame crow that you previously ignored
Till you come to a doorway: a girl is waiting with a cigarette burn on
    her forehead
And little toes extrude from the too narrow flipflops,
And you walk on past, into the outskirts, open fields still escaping
    construction work
And a woman shouts a question to you from across the field at
    midday,

A question not usually framed in these terms, like a vendor of
    newspapers or fish
(A question even Dr Weisshorn had been unable to frame) –
But which hangs there in its simplicity in the midday heat
Shimmering like the bright star of a migraine
Or the chiselled lines of a poem you are not going to read.

The nightingales have not made a sound
As the sky darkens across the river.
A young rabbit runs over a field towards a hedge.
Nightingales will imitate other birds,
Even other nightingales with the wrong accent.
Originally called *nightinglass*
They held the night in schooners of sherry.

Madeline has gone into moon therapy by the way.
You become aware of the moon
As a gravitational presence, like a massive elder sister
Trundling beside you just out of sight.
And the moon imagines the earth as the home of lost objects
As you look back from the top of a bus going towards Victoria
At a shop selling lost umbrellas.

Then on comes Emily Brontë – Hello Emily, I say
How are things up at Haworth? – Oh, she says,
They're OK. It's a bit wild up here of course
And Father's in one of his moods and Keeper
Seems to have got hardpad. I really feel
I must get out of this place. There's nothing to do.
I get up at ten these days. There's been a revolution.
Heathcliff brings me my breakfast in bed. Can you imagine?
I really wish he wouldn't but there you are. We get
What we deserve. It's going to be a poor summer
For harebells. The window in the spare bedroom
Needs repairing. I'm going through a lot of stuff
I wrote as a child in the attic. It's embarrassing
But I can't bring myself to throw it away. Well that's all really.
There's no news. Linton's taken up the guitar.
Nelly spends a lot of time in the scullery doing the pools.
It gives her an interest. We've had the Belling
Taken out and replaced with a Hotpoint.
She's taken to it well. Apart from that nothing.
There's ice hockey on TV which Father's taken a surprising interest
   in.
It takes him away from his sermons. Sometimes I think
He's going to turn into an Existentialist.
Well let him. It'll be no skin off anyone's nose here.
Charlotte got some hashish from a man in Leeds
And smokes it quite openly in the writing room

The mind, gentlemen, is a small midlands town, like Kettering
Where they made corsets for years
And the giant factory dominates the scene.
As you pass by on the train
You especially notice the word CORSETS
In the fine confident lettering of the period
And although corsets are not required any more
It still goes on producing them
Because that is what it does, that is what it is.

The soul is a quite different town
Whose name escapes me, further north,
Where they made curtain-like material in large sheets
That were hung out to dry in strips,
Long as the hair of a princess,
Long as cricket pitches,
From specially constructed high balconies
Till the damp strips, like seaweed, congealed into linoleum
Ready to hang over the moon
In long rolls with beige stripes
And Greek key patterns.

THE MISSED APPOINTMENT

Dear Mr S.
I was sorry not to see you in clinic yesterday.
Your only message was a faint noise that woke me at 4 this morning
Like wings being folded in darkness
And a breath on the pillow close to my ear.
I understand you were upset about the possible reunion
photographs
Prior to the celebration cycle race and broke your spectacles
Because they contained images of the past.
You said, 'Some people make the journey: others did not.'
We must leave it at that I think. I appreciate your attempt
To get in touch in the hours of darkness
With the tiny almost inaudible noises
And trust they were not ironic.
Please feel free to resume contact at any time
Perhaps on some windswept moor.
Sent unsigned to avoid delay.
PS I woke with my left hand trembling so much
I could hardly strap on my watch.

SHOULD CATULLUS BE READ
BY OLD PEOPLE?

But it says in my booklet here
(Delivered through the door by the Council
And illustrated in watercolour)
That older people also need sexual activity,
May even enjoy it. Have the proclivity. Along with bowls etc.
No need for expensive uniforms, shields or padding
It's just a matter of engaging each other
Enough, with enough cream, while pretending to be young
With the lights out. Though we could use pen torches for reassurance.
And if you die they resuscitate you
Saying there's romance in you yet.

And another thing, they say
Don't fight shy of the latest variation.
At least attempt it once a week. (Thursday for example.)
It's perfectly normal among gazelles apparently.

We had this girl come round, nicely spoken, very good shoes, wore
    a pashmina.
Put us at our ease. Not the council, community outreach.
(Under the same umbrella with a smaller footprint).
To expand our horizons.

I broached the topic with Madge afterwards
But she didn't seem over the moon.
I had enough trouble getting her to switch off the Hoover.
But if you're resistant to change they think you belong in remedial.
The woman's coming back next week for an update. Says to keep a
    diary.
So I broached the topic as I said with Madge.
There's some things you can't press. She's the same with Brussels
    sprouts.

('Very nice dear I'm sure'.)
It was hard enough to get her to change to a flex account.
I remembered getting Monty to take an interest in Pedigree Chum.
But we have to have something to put in the diary.

Where were we? Yes. Catullus.
All this Lesbia.
Could an Italian be interested in one woman with a name like that
    for so long?
Monkish scribes put Lesbia if they saw Cynthia
Like censors in the war. ('Do you really want to say this?')
And readdress love letters when the man is writing to more than two
Women at once and mixed up the envelopes
Which Catullus was bound to
Because in both letters the interesting bits
Were out of Sappho. I read this book
By a German or Frenchman (anyway continental
Probably French, a typical French story)
About this Russian helping a Frenchman with his love life.
He said Just get some love poems and
Love letters (doesn't matter where from
Or who has written them) and copy them
And send them. That's all you have to do.
Week after week. She won't read them
But she'll get used to receiving them.
Catullus: half his copy cribbed from Sappho, sent
To Glycera, Drusilla, Beryl etc.
And the other half (rude but sincere)
Was by monks scribbling in the margins.
There was nothing else to do in the fourteenth century.
Imagine it: first you're in the fourteenth century
(That's the 1300s remember)
Then, on top of that, you're Philip Larkin in a cowl.
It's enough to make you want to spray things on trains.

1.

Her made to measure mental camisole
Fluffed out a little at the edges, holds
Suggestions of Byzantium, in green.
Its acrobatic hemlines, year by year,
Trace with acutest sighs a *mappemonde*.
Phenomenal cadenzas of the real!
She dreams of crystal *vol au vents*, and sings
Miming the waxy cadence of pale fruit
And feels eternal in her *crêpe de chine*.

Louche lingeries of logic! Beige on beige
Philosophies the texture of brioche
Hold with faint exhalations Marimonde
Who walks parterres of velvet, pondering,
And longs for vaguer jabots, looser tulle.

2.

Her modishly hermetic camisole
Fluffed out a little at the edges, holds
The Platonists perplexed at the last green.
She traces with her sighs a *mappemonde*'s
Fanatical fandangos on the real.
Her beige on beige, her metamorphic green
Suggest the postulation of some green
Confection, of some philosophic brioche
That tempts with crisp susurrus Marimonde
(Emerging now in impertinent camisole)
To dream of crystal *vol au vents*, and sing
Of long Laforgue-style *jabots*, softer tulle,
And mime the waxy softness of pale fruit
And feel eternal in her *crêpe de chine*.

3.

Fernickety cadenzas! Café Royal!
Why should they bother us, those half-flexed thighs
Purporting to contain a *mappemonde*?
She sinks her teeth in a platonic brioche.
The pouting tulle, veloured anatomies,
Burgeoning *bergeres'* hypostatic green!
The longed-for Vogue-in-jackboots lassitude!
Hermetic whispers from the camisole
Are all we ask of logic and its norms.
Byzantium's fluffy *vol au vents*, its dreams
Of picturing the post-conceptual green
Are philosophic hemlines, year by year,
That mime the unrotting texture of wax fruit
And feel eternal in their *crêpe de chine*.

4.

The modiste's hermeneutic commissar
Fluffing his whiskers at the edges, holds
A mirror up to every last colleen.
He dresses with his eyes Miss Lovibond's
Conception of herself as Comte de L'Isle.
His fashion page, hermaphroditic green,
Shows an impastoed Asian in some green
Confusion with a fellow-sapphic Bosche.
The tent is crisp, the sisters, moribund,
Imagine how the importunate commissar
Daydreams of Christ-like elevations, sings
Of long Laforgue-style jabots, softer tulle,
And mines the soft recesses of peeled fruit
And feels eternal as a Balanchine.

5·

Her moodily paraded commissure
Fluffed out a little at the edges, holds
A mirror to the other's Halloween.
Funambulistic vistas of the real!
Philosophy becomes a blue tureen
We bob for apples in. Sir Alfred Mond
A Shadrak volunteering to be singed.
She spurns the proferred chocolate of male fruit
And feels eternal in her *crepe de chine*.

Logic's black mannequins have left the stage.
Philosophy's a large horsehair barouche
That lulls in its exhaustion Marimonde
To sleep in velvet garages, to dream
Of ever silkier pistons, tyres of tulle.

6. *(quasi giocoso)*

The apocalyptic ocean's *crepe de chine*
Half hides the swollen bodies of the saints.
Fluffed out a little at the edge, it holds
A waste of taffetas, soiled bombazine
As layette for a stillborn faery queen.
Byzantium's garden city year by year
Extends its parks, but traffic won't abscond.
The Platonists go chase their jumping bean:
The ocean hardly yields a conger eel.
Feeling autumnal in his *crèpe de chine*
Philosophy has donned a gabardine
And tempts a child with greasy Murraymints
To walk parterres of velvet, pondering
On ever vaguer jabots, looser tulle.

7.

SS Byzantium's mess deck green
Is quite an adornment to the holiday scene:
You put your face through a hole in the screen
And scowling at the camera year by year
As if the Sea of Azov were a pond.
Imagine summer long as a Eugene
O'Neill trilogy. The wife hides in the wings
In her disguise a Leonid Massine
And smoking for the nonce a beige cheroot
She feels eternal as a balance sheet.
She's older than the wrecks. I'll have a spritz.
The Platonist has vanished for a nosh
Still boxing with the wind and La Gioconde
And takes a giblet with his Jethro Tull

8

Beneath a voucher for an Attic frieze
Philosophers dissect the slouching Beast.
The technique is matchless: it's a barcarole
That tinkles round box hedges and unfolds
In circumambient clouds of *extra fine*
Faint hints to students, tier on questing tier,
Who score each grace note, trying not to sneeze,
And underline BYZANTIUM in green.
It's the tone of voice that draws them like a weir:
The exit lines are 30 denier, sheer
Drops down the skislopes of Romantic Art.
Ah, Marimonde! My visa for the East!
A carefree tampon in its bleeding heart
The problem of pain slides down your glittering *piste.*

9. *Questionnaire*

What is going on here? Does the poet's jocular tone
Get on your nerves? Can he bear to be alone?
What is the colour of her telephone?
Describe the scene in words of your own.
Who is Professor Dawson? Is he well known?

10. *Appendix*

The identity of the ever-elusive figure
Of the middle sonnets has long been an enigma
To critics. Professor Dawson said he'd be jiggered
If he could fathom it, and that no stigma
Should attach to any worthwhile student
Who came out frankly as he did. There was no information.
There were younger heads, among whom the imprudent
Plumped for a libellous identification
With Dawson himself. Others saw her in more complex terms
According to their grants and disciplines.
One saw her as a Marxist palinode
Another spent Michaelmas and Easter terms
Pricking her image with dressmaker's pins.
For one whole summer she was quite the mode.

When we sang Tosca uncentralheated
And crouching together for warmth on all fours
Beneath two layers of double duvet

Or rather I was singing and you listened and joined in
There was no need to search for a voice
As they tell you to do in *How to Write a Novel*.

The garden gate creaked of its own accord
And she fell into my arms, so that *quasi parlando*
Occurred as if spontaneously

And the invisible man who listens every night
From the wardrobe, peering through the slats
At intimate moments, what did he see?

And the novels glancing askance
From their faded jackets?
Did it speak to them, the muffled *vagamente?*

How could it speak to any of us in No 27
Or in the small front garden of the terrace?
There was hardly a garden gate to creak.

No precinct to be invaded
By a footfall. How then did it happen
This break in the voice, so Blair-like you even laughed?

Doreen looked back at me, her face like a Tacitus unseen.
I like difficult poets who tease you, difficult girls
Pulling their hair over their faces and running away.
Though this could get tiresome.
Soon it will be time to cycle through the rain to yoga.
I wish I was mysterious.
All I wanted was to be opaque and cryptic.
Later perhaps arcane.
Was that too much to hope for?
Who wants a Delphic oracle who says what she means?
I left our church because they prayed in English
And went to Roman mass down the road, till I learnt Latin
And had to go to the next street where mass was in Polish.
When I began to pick up a few words of that language
I left for a guru who gave me a meaningless sound.
When that suggested a wave on a tropical beach
I had to leave and go to yoga classes.
Everything is fine now. I can't understand a word.

At twenty-five, Mutus thought that embarking on a second affair –
(Though 'embarkation' was hardly the word, suggesting
A flurry of cabin trunks, nautical cries, hawsers, tides and
gangplanks,
And calling to mind, as many things did,
His parents' picture of *A Voyage to Cythera*
In the downstairs cloakroom) –
Would be like having a second slice of cake
Or learning a new language, or going on
To some kind of higher education, as if
Proceeding from algebra to trigonometry
Or from Base Camp to the North Face.
No disrespect to algebra, it could even be a logical step.
Or taking out a new book from Boots Lending Library
So that he could walk slowly along the crest of the road
Avoiding the camber on either side,
His head buried in the text of a new plot,
Ignoring all the traffic, and with the bookmark
From Boots Lending Library swinging slowly like a pendulum
As he walked.

Sometimes, although we never pray, because
It doesn't work and we don't believe in magic,
We feel it would be nice to be one of those
People who say their prayers, and so may buy

An icon from a shop in Florence
In a distressed gilt frame (made by
The Fratelli Alinari). And there's this Madonna
With a face like an egg looking at you with

That slightly unfocussed expression.
At midnight, though our lives are irretrievable,
I get out of bed and kneel a moment
(I could say I was looking for my slippers).

After his restraining order, Henry
Still follows Maureen about from day to day
Stalking her shadow as if she could show up
In two places at once like St Francis of Assisi
In the Waitrose carpark, or the filling station.
Yet when after a period of vacuous fantasy
Like an unending run of *Blithe Spirit*
She cycles towards him smiling in the park
He marches on past, like a soldier going over the top,
Or a man with his head immobilised
In the vice of some Victorian photographer
Against a background of palms and columns,
And in his mind tiny crossed swords
Marking an old battle in an ordnance survey map.

I cultivated the higher melancholy
Leopardi was on my shelf and in my heart.
I could recite eight lines.
Father, fearing I'd become a nancy-boy,
Had iron horseshoes fixed to the heels of my suedes.
I felt like a centaur as I clopped in my career
Through libraries and bedrooms
Making a slow crisp ringing sound
Like a Captain of Horseguards
At a state funeral. All I needed was spurs.
People could hear me coming like a leper.
The tell-tale clank as I climbed her fire escape
Gave the Italian girl time to hide in the wardrobe
Leaving only her shoes behind.
I frowned into the wardrobe mirror, murmuring, *'in noi di cari*
  inganni'
In a pretty good accent
Derived from three weeks in Perugia.
Leopardi cut no ice with the customs man in Rome
And did not help me here.
She knew there was something wrong
When I offered to carry her handbag.
Later, introduced to her Uncle on the Lido,
I clicked my heels and bowed slightly
Like a Nazi in a film.
Her Uncle, who'd made a fortune in cement
Propping up Venice, was not impressed
When I told him I was studying Etruscan.
It was, he said, the fashion.
Returning to England, I phoned Deirdre:
'How about you can be Walter Pater, I'll be the Grand Canal?'

At this stage in the war, Hitler
Had walled up Goering
Under the Alps
Together with Piero della Francesca.
We read *Prediction* weekly
And looked more to the future in those days.
J.W. Dunne had proved
That time could go backwards
Provided you stayed asleep in a railway carriage
With your back to the engine. Scott's Emulsion
Helped you walk to the North Pole
And you knew it was nerve gas
If it smelt like geraniums.
A blond German boy
Came into the kitchen to ask for a nailbrush.
People were more cheerful in those days
And we had them in for drinks.
Even old Mr Hebble
Who'd lost both his sons in the Battle of Britain
Said, 'I'll have a port and brandy thank you Brenda.'

JUNK MAIL

Despite your long silence, I write again.
I appreciate that you are dead, but even so
You could light a candle in that other room
And I would come to you singing like Jonas Kaufmann
Demonstrating a controlled diminuendo
On a high E natural. If we were spirits
I wouldn't have to wash. And that intimate sigh
Into the ear, that wakes me at midnight –
Is it really from the orthopaedic mattress?
Or do they have ventriloquists where you are?
It is possible to fall in love with a woman.
There are people who have fallen in love with a postage stamp.
Fortunes have been left to cats
Who never spoke a word and never will.

HAWK MOULTING

The poets are out watching hawks again.
They can't get enough of it.
They crick their necks looking upwards
And spin round and get dizzy and fall over.
They are ringing shearwaters on the Isle of Uist in the dark.
What is it about poultry?
A necessary apprenticeship or preliminary fieldwork
That will allow them to proceed to poetry itself.
Their mentors are old crofters speaking Gaelic.
What are they going to do next?
Work in a bird hospital
Mending the wings, the flight feathers all with their peculiar names.
They join emergency teams with trolleys scooting along wards
Filled with hoopoes, bitterns, behind curtains
Whooping and crying, some hysterical,
Others with genuine fortitude.

He looms at the end of the corridor
Like a discarded muff, or
A guardsman coming up through the floorboards.
There's something sinister
About the way he looks at you
Turning his short sighted eyes up and sideways
Baring his teeth in the scared grin
Of a priest who thinks you have caught him having lewd thoughts.
He cringes electrically when you try and stroke him,
A new member of some encounter group.
His musky smell fills the house
Like the armpit of a newly bathed and aroused woman
But unable to seduce.
He climbs the louvre window like a glacier:
All he wants to do is get away.
But we must have him out of his brown study
Clattering over the wood floor like a badly trained platoon
To sit on the bookcase
Holding a German sausage in his changeling claws.
Even the cat respects him
Instinctively shy of his excessive non violence.
He's the one who never speaks in the therapy group. We suspect
The shrunken ears of the priest who has heard too much.
All he does is sneeze
And even that with his hands in front of his face like an old lady.
He is the silent woman in some lost play
Who dominates the stage.
Upside down in the trees
He becomes his own hammock but
He's under the bed now,
A chamberpot dressed up in a monkey suit
That they used to put children's pyjamas in. We call him opossum

But hereabouts they call him *'kuskus'*
(Bureaucrat, clerk, one who makes his living
By writing).

THE TAMER SHORES OF LOVE

I saw her coming out of Tesco's,
The hair recalling ancient frescoes.
– Fiona! I called, You look just the same!
'The Tamer Shores of Love'? ... As tame?

– I can't ... recall your context.
– But what about me?
– Could you be... Professor Unbegaun by any chance?
– Unbegaun? He was lost at sea.
Dragged down by Russian poetry.
And sleeps beside the sleepless cod
Beneath the sea of Novgorod.

Years later, she's slithering from a taxi.
Her frock is labelled Cotopaxi.
– Fiona! I called, Noctambulant simian!
How was Egypt? And the Sphinx?

Have they got a decent links?
She shuffles her harness.—I'm with Damien.
You're not... Professor Unbegaun?
– Well yes I am! I'm back in town!
– How's poetry? And Novgorod?
– The amoeba has a pseudopod
That helps it limp towards its God.
And I will find my Novgorod.

And there is Furlough holding up a lamp
That's blinking on and off like Holman Hunt
Or Florence Nightingale as if it can't decide
Whether to go on or off, fuse or explode,
And I half turn from the socket and look up
At Furlough standing on a table
His face lit flickering like an apparition
Of Christ knocking at the door of the human heart
And I say – Shall I switch it *orf?*
(Pronouncing off to rhyme with Castle Corfe, or dwarf.)
I'm thinking – Why not try it? It's an opportunity.
I'd already managed *lorst* to rhyme with divorced.
And I admire Furlough – (a physicist who speaks Italian
And can draw electric circuits and make fire balloons
And play the lute and his sister lives in Rome –)
And I'm thinking (as one does at such moments)
– If I can get away with *orf*
People may think my parents don't live in Leicester
But in Eaton Square like Schlotterman's
Or go otter-hunting in Devon like Furze-Parsling's.
But I see from Furlough's half-smile
That I will not be trying this again
In my lifetime. I remember this more clearly
Than my first love, or the deaths of my parents.

In another room as she was putting on snowboots
– (Confiscated from a lodger who had not paid any rent
Being a Marxist who rode off on a Ducati)
Deirdre was singing to herself unconsciously
Thinking of the lodger without his snowboots at the South Pole
Searching for lichens – and the singing
Was like a cello but very light and high and went on and on
Like that cello piece that they often play
Insistently as background to some conversation
Between detectives in Sweden
So that you can hardly hear it and are hardly
Aware of it in the background like a mountain stream
As you are listening to the complex conversation
About some corpse found or lost in a wood in Sweden or Willesden
And then you become aware that this music which you had always
    loved
Was going on and you preferred to hear it because it was almost
    inaudible,
and longed for it to go on,
Rather than the increasingly complex and austere conversation
    between the detectives.
And the voice, relaxed, unforced, higher than you'd have thought
    possible
(So high, too high even for the cello really, and no time to take
    breath,
As her voice, certainly her singing voice, had never been soprano)
And I casually went into that room for something
And put my hand on her shoulder for a moment
As she gradually finished lacing up her snowboots.

She never really let me have a proper go, Shirley.
There was always the frozen inch as Mr Cattermole called it.
You could tell from the way she sat on the couch
Crossing her legs with a straight back, sitting diagonally,
And holding the handbag as if for the front page of *Country Life.*
The higher you got the colder it was.
You couldn't help thinking of Shackleton and his ponies. Ice in the
      rigging.
If only he'd used dogs like Amundsen.
He'd be home and dry. But what was home and dry
Compared to the sepia photographs of Cape Desolation
The tattered rigging, the boat caught fast in ice?
Icicles horizontal in the wind?
I decided to get a butler's sink installed in the kitchenette
So she might think my people had once owned a butler.

I wake with a hand on the insane root.
The usual stalky tuberose slack polypoid mass
Like something you might find on a beach at low tide.
You could imagine Osbert Sitwell poking it cautiously with his stick
In his wanderings at low tide in Scarborough out of season.
And thinking it could be gathered and delivered
in bales as a mulch. To protect and nourish gardens.
Crawling with white sand hoppers. A sea cucumber.
You could hang it up and tell the weather by it.
Though the weather would never be the same as it was in
Scarborough.
And B. held it one night in the palm of her hand
While falling asleep gradually as an infant in its cot
Falls asleep at last holding a small wooden farm animal,
A sheep perhaps, and gradually opens its hand as sleep descends.

RUMPELSTILSTSKIN REFLECTS

Others before were non-events (John Donne).

So that made it OK? .

What happened to the wild duck in the end?

Write the story from the wild duck's point of view.

His laughter sounded hollow in the bedroom.

Four in the morning. In China they'd be having tea.

In nineteenth century Russia they'd still be starting lunch at three
    in the afternoon.

There were such things as solitary bees.

Herons managed on one leg.

What spider has not eaten its mother?

The heron stands at a curve in the ditch in the swampy field

Hunched up, back to the wind, studying Sanskrit.

– Write a poem about me.

Every night. Keep a notebook under your pillow.

'Love,' she says later,
When we are alone in the lounge
After looking round the plastic rose factory,
'No one can have too much love. Don't you agree?
When it hits you, it's like a drug
And you get to know where to find it.'
Death was always in her mind.
Reincarnation? A butterfly was a bit of a cul de sac.
'I believe in existentialism, in freedom, in developing one's talents.
How many wives did Mao have? Four?
Not many. Not many at all. Whatever Dr Wigston might say.'
Personally she believed in boarding school.
She dreamed so much. It was healthy to dream wasn't it?
In Kathmandu, the young priestess had drunk the blood
spurting from the neck. She had wanted to sit down.
At the souvenir shop one went straight for the blue shirts.
Larger size, her breasts would only be accentuated.
She let them have her wallet. There.
Mao's house, was it for sale?
It was enchanting. An enchanting little place. With the lotus pond.
She was looking round for another house.
One needed so much less as one grew older, or she hoped so.
Of course we were eating lotus here,
Often without knowing it. That rooty thing.
Could she get a Mao jacket?
Or would it take too long to get it made?
When she got back from the Amazon people in Copenhagen said
Why don't you take those jungle boots off?
Some say one is reincarnated every moment.
Personally she would like to be an English sheepdog.
(*In the corridor, a chambermaid is singing. Her clear soprano.*)

That old man on the rooftop doing tai chi,
Fluent and radiant as an angel. Who would believe that?
They would say she was overwrought.
She used to be so amusing,
Now she is serious. But she was serious.
She tried out herself, her reality,
What was life all about? What could Denmark reply? Bacon and
    Kierkegaard?
Perhaps she would find the answer this afternoon, in the Han
    Tombs
Like E.M. Forster, someone would put his hand on her bottom.
She had had that experience before, it must be something beyond
    that
At her age. How many tombs would she have to visit?
It was all so very long ago, the Lady Chang-O flying to the moon.

It was Monday morning already.
The peignoir had been slept in all night
And the cockatoo had left a green mess on the rug
Before being eaten by the cat, it seemed.
I was not going to buy Big Issue today.
Where was home after all?
Even the angels shivered in their tombs.
I put on a sensible dressing gown and ran a bath.
Then went downstairs and watched a pineapple

– Just live your own life. I don't mind. Aren't you wasting your time?
– But anything else is a waste of time.
– It's not love it's like margarine.
– But you're not listening to me. You never listen.
In the street, people nimbly avoid each other's mobiles.
At the Executive Club in Alpha Road
The wood-nymphs are sweeping up and disenchanting themselves
Cleaning their faces with moist towels
Grimacing sideways into small mirrors.
Garages and chemists are rolling up chain link fences
Owls are settling softly into their nests.
The queue for fish is starting at the corner.
Shopkeepers are putting out their awnings.
Aubergines are being polished.
Yogis are rolling up their mats.
Old ladies in Chesterton Hall Crescent are switching on the news.
And I am writing about you Glynis as if it was still midnight
Using an old diary for 1996 and pretending to forget your name
Or where you lived or to mix you up with the other one so I felt like
    Virgil
Invoking a flighty wood nymph
With long erudite divagations and calling different names,
Waving long divagations in the air like a magician waving a very
    long scarlet silk scarf
In zigzags. Whether you go by the name of Daphne now,
And are wandering the night clubs of Dewsbury
Or are being worshipped perhaps under the name of Briony or Mrs
    Huckstep
By simple peasants in their remote indigenous settlements,
Or it could be you are wandering barefoot over rocks at Scarborough
Or pursuing bears in the forests of Alberta
With your husband who has a licence to do this.

Perhaps you are fleeing an incestuous uncle in Harrogate
Or in the form of a plant stretch wayward tendrils
Over the rusting ironwork of Brighton pier...
If you are loitering by the deserted tennis courts of Carisbrooke
    Road
Listening to the strains of the last waltz by Gerry Flanagan and his
    city slickers
While couples disappear through French windows into the
    darkness,
Or you are striding barefoot again over the turd-hazardous
    parkland of Newnham
Or rolling headlong in sunlight down the grassy incline opposite St
    Genny's.
You may be grabbing the steering wheel of the Nissan Micra as it
Negotiates a hairpin bend in the Dolomites.
Listen Dilys, whether you are trailing your high heeled foot to
    describe a giant comma
On the floor of the tango lounge at St Paul's,
Or coming in late to yoga class in wide Turkish trousers,
Or in scarlet running shorts racing over sea cliffs
Like a tiny seal on a Chinese landscape,
Or running in tears beneath the tall yew hedges of the asylum
Or watching Aztec figures dancing on the ceiling in McKenzie Road,
While a mattress is thrown out of the window, bringing the
    guttering with it,
Listen to me Phyllis.
No. You listen to me.
Listen to me for a change.

THE EYE TEST

I don't want to see too much.
I would like to see Doreen in the half light by the fence
Close up smelling of creosote
Feeling her scratch my palm in the moonlight
If there was moonlight.
Just a rough image would be quite enough
I'm not asking for detail or long distance.
Otherwise I can just smell creosote.
I can see some people clear as crystal but have no idea who they are.
I don't want to see Nurse Creeley.
I don't want to see Dr Felucca unless he's fallen into a pond.
I don't want to see Tamsin's husband too close
But would rather see him slightly further away..

Will she come do you think? He's all of a dangle
Again, the ginseng makes his hair curl
And when she pulls her trousers up over her knees she's a lexicon
Of unusual meanings for the word chums.

He's having a bath in case she comes.
What a way to spend Sunday morning, thinking of Mexico
And its unpronounceable names. The youngest Chalet girl
Is sketching Amadis de Gaula in the jungle.

An arborescent sarcophagus shrinks to a rectangle
As intricate nose-flutes skirl
Through the blue frost of Oaxaca
And Montezuma's entourage succumbs.

Crescendo on carotid drums
As Cortes tries to get his armour off: his eczema
Itchy as a broken record of the erl-
King, jockeyed by the quangle-wangle.

We may hope she comes. Her corybantic ankle
In its striped sock could unfurl
A pomological revolution under plexiglass
And lead to the development of new plums.

– And your husband?
– My husband specialises in the photography of raindrops
On the faces of moonlit young girls
Of fair complexion and in ragged clothes
Climbing up ivy-clad gothic walls
Of windswept church towers in Norfolk
To the accompaniment of Bach's D minor Toccata.
– And so... you thought –?
– Well, we heard the appeal on the radio
About this girl who was trapped in some way
Half way up an ivy-clad wall
While being photographed for some soap advertisement
('Raindrop' soap, they said)
Unable to get up or down. So I called the number
And spoke with the husband (or purported)
And he gave me the code details and I came down immediately
As we, my husband and I, might have the expertise
To get up and down in this situation,
Being bona fide investigators, not prurient.
We are not religious people, though open to persuasion.
All the lights had gone out except for one neoplatonic gleam.

Fogarty introduced us to the Eighteenth Century
By telling me not to say Pitt brought up a bill
As it was like saying the cat brought up its breakfast.
It put me off History altogether. I couldn't see
Why we needed to study Americans
Now they claimed to be independent.
Let them study their own history.
They'd only themselves to blame.
He made me write, 'I am not one of the 7 dwarves:
I do not whistle while I work' 500 times
Though Baden Powell said boys should whistle all the time.
Fogarty's handwriting, with its weird undecipherable Greek ms
Was like the desperate fingernail scratches of a girl kidnapped
And locked in the boot of a car.

BUILDING A HERB GARDEN: FOGIE'S DRIFT

Old man's drivel
(*Garrulopedia senex*)
Locally known as Fogie's drift
'Revels on abandoned altars.
Under the dominion of Saturn'.
Glabrous and sessile
It can present a threatening appearance
On moonlit nights beneath a sitting room window.
It enjoyed a vogue in thirties flower arrangements
On top of boudoir grand pianos
With its cataracts of foaming umber.
In October it tends to get brown and sad.
In November it falls over and ideally should be rotted down.

Mr McPherson could never expect to be popular.
He occupied the New Block, for Mathematics,
Built by some reluctant afterthought
Beyond Museum and Stinks.
Plywood tea-chests for waste paper
(Crumpled love notes and old log tables)
Dominated the cement floors, while as you came in,
A print of Botticelli's *Primavera*
Offered the illusion of escape.
Summer sunlight streamed in through the window.
McPherson was never at ease with himself,
Still less with the external world.
When he went berserk, which was not unusual,
Flecks of beige foam would curdle around his lips
Like brackish sediment round an intertidal rock pool.
My friend Olsen, a physicist,
Was keen to photograph this phenomenon.
My task was to bait the master by odd questions,
While Olsen lurked behind a pile of Greek lexicons
Loosely arranged like a birdwatcher's hide.
– But sir-
– What is it boy?
– I'm not happy about tan theta sir.
– Clariston and Dainty. Page 18...
– Unless the tower is leaning over sir.
Or is it a reflection in the lake?
Should I be leaning backwards?
– Open your Clariston and Dainty. Page 18.
– But sir.
– What is it now boy?
– Sir. Mr Templeton says sir. It's more important
For a proposition to be interesting than to be true.

Does that mean Maths is like Art sir?
If so, should we have a cheese plant in the corner?
The Leica clicked. Swinging round, McPherson
Swept Olsen off his desk with a single blow.
– Fetch the waste bin. Open the door. Stand back.
I don't want anyone else to get hurt.
I'm going to boot this boy out of the room.
Willing hands obeyed. Olsen's head
Was forced down among the love notes
As he bent double like a hinge.
The metal strips reinforcing the plywood
Shrieked protest as they chafed against the cement,
As kick by kick the chest lurched forward.
Above us, the Graces continued their enigmatic dance
Beneath the enchanted trees.

I overtook a hearse the other day.
I was in a hurry. It was in my way.
It hooted and started tailgating.
The more dead they are the faster they want to go.
Trying to make up for lost time.
The girl at the bank asked me what I planned
To do with all my money. They do that nowadays.
I told her the Pre-Socratics were my Mills and Boon.
My only phone calls were from British Gas
And if they failed to call I felt lonely.
They only wanted to talk to my wife.
I told them not to call again. She was away.
But the man, who seemed quite pleasant (Irish)
Didn't seem in a hurry, and keeps calling again.
Even at six pm when I'm in the bath
After a hard day doing nothing.
The phone goes. I can tell it's him.
He can't explain why he wants to call.
Like some gentle detective or therapist
He didn't seem to have anyone else to phone
And pretended to be a bit hesitant.
It could be an offer of some kind
Or a solution to the Riemann hypothesis.
When young I'd ring up random numbers
And make insulting remarks and hang up.
These people are coming back to haunt you.
I don't suppose he's Irish at all.
A job like that, you're practising accents.
I googled frottage yesterday.
And immediately got a colour zoom in
Of two penises like heraldic animals.
So I switched off and unplugged in case police

Would say I'm downloading inappropriate menus.
I was looking for Max Ernst
But wouldn't recognise him by his penis any more than Cézanne.
It's mixed media at our Art Group
And Diane says
She's introducing frottage to her scrabble team.
(She's from New Zealand)
She says it's what French people do
When brass rubbing in old country churches.

END OF LIFE PLAN

1

In the run-up to my end of life plan (EOLP)
I have an appointment at 0940
With a travel agent. On Thursday.
No, Friday, Friday. I'm booked
With Bronwen Callaghan, G.P.. I could have had anyone:
The man behind the desk
Asked me who I'd like. I wasn't in a hurry.
I wasn't looking for an assassin. And even if I was
I'd prefer someone I didn't know.
But I'll have a GP because they don't listen anyway.
Why should they listen?
They don't have Death now. Only End of Life.
John Donne was right, though he always exaggerated.
So he puts me down with Bronwen.
It's Thursday already. I don't think up last words.

I'd like to die in the school play
Cast as Romeo, in Leichner's 5&9
Against Tony McCulloch Captain of Boxing
As Juliet, in a wig, seeing me apparently dead
And collapsing on top of me in the sarcophagus
So I feel his bristly chin against my cheek.
My parents in the front row. Mum in the ocelot.
And I'm not even dead.

2

Or put it another way
If I could talk my way out of the play
By closing the conversation with a sigh
(Don't sigh! It's unlucky to sigh!)
I'm just breathing deeply. I need oxygen.

3

Death is not a Portuguese voyage in 1498
Although it might have been at the time.
Nor would we think it amiss to speak of the grand fair
Which the natives call *Gunxineu Apparau*
Xinanguibaleu. That is to say
Rich fair of the prison of the condemned.

4

And now she thought of death abstractedly
As a crumpled receipt she had left in the handbag
Somewhere without thinking who might need it.
In any case with the lawn in that tussocky condition
They should give her some time. If she thought of death
It would be as a terminus like Paddington
Surrounded by those wretched little hotels.

5

Do you have a belief system at all?
Not that we mind. It's just that it can be nice
To have something you can do in a group setting.

6.

On Channel 4, moribund elephants
Seek the place their parents died
And caress the old skulls feelingly with their trunks.
We generally go to Blakeney.

Mr Penge sharpened his gramophone needles by hand.
They were wooden, I think beechwood or elm,
And needed to be sharpened with a special knife,
And could produce from his machine with its horn
Sharp or soft focus sounds as if from an Ouija board
Depending on how much he had sharpened the needle
Which he did every day before the performance
As if making a fresh cup of coffee.
Well suited to the misty exhalations of Debussy
Dans une brume doucement profonde
And to the mysteries of Mallarmé
He chalked up on the board *LE VIERGE, LE VIVACE...*
Like an obscure timetable for a foreign train
That no one was going to get onto and which would never arrive –
A tall abstracted man more scholar than housemaster
Like a missionary priest who finds himself in command of a man of
     war.
When I was kicking open the door of the dormitory as usual on a
     summer afternoon
He would be standing on the other side. Or when I signed a chit for
     razorblades
He would inquire *Shaving or suicide?*
He said I took myself too seriously.
He was encouraging us in the virtues of irony.
Penge's voice was like some antique wind instrument
With an obscure name, like a court-bassoon,
His favourite phrase, (much imitated) was
'In actual point of fact.'

So I'm lying there on the beach reading a magazine
And two male nudes are playing Frisbee.
One of them stands right close over me like this
'Want a game of Frisbee?' And I say (after a pause, brightly)

'No thanks.' I go in the café. There's a girl
(All the girls were stunningly beautiful, from France,
Germany mostly) – sitting at a table
Immaculately groomed, maybe lets part of a dress fall

To show a bit, you know, just a little
Then puts her head forward into the soup and ravels all her hair
And tosses it back to make it look dishevelled.
It was, you know, all right.

You had to have the dishevelled look in Bali.
And the good looking men, Adonis style,
A bit too good looking, you know?
A little bit too much body sway for Frisbee throwing.

I must give you back the Thomas Hardy book
Before it gets covered in yoghurt.

MY FATHER AT PRAYER

To save time in the mornings
Father used to say his prayers
While doing a headstand on the bathroom rug
Close to the Baxi convector heater
And attended by familiar reading matter:
A catalogue of clothes worn by the Royal Family
And, slightly further away, Behannon's *Yoga*
Open at the photograph illustrating
Isolation of the left rectus abdominis
(A bearded fakir looking half embalmed),
Spread out on the blue linoleum.
Maintaining this inverted position
He would read aloud from *The Nun's Prayer*:
'Lord, Thou knowest I am no longer young,'
Swaying slightly, he brought to mind
A girl tottering on six-inch heels,
Bringing out protective instincts.
In this position, nobody could approach him
And even death seemed for a while disarmed.